USING COMPUTERS

Machine with a Mouse

Based on the Math Monsters™ public television series, developed in cooperation with the National Council of Teachers of Mathematics (NCTM).

by John Burstein

Reading consultant: Susan Nations, M.Ed., author/literacy coach/consultant

Math curriculum consultants: Marti Wolfe, M.Ed., teacher/presenter; Kristi Hardi-Gilson, B.A., teacher/presenter

WEEKLY WR READER®
EARLY LEARNING LIBRARY

Please visit our web site at: **www.earlyliteracy.cc**
For a free color catalog describing Weekly Reader® Early Learning Library's list
of high-quality books, call 1-877-445-5824 (USA) or 1-800-387-3178 (Canada).
Weekly Reader® Early Learning Library's fax: (414) 336-0164.

Library of Congress Cataloging-in-Publication Data

Burstein, John.
      Using computers: machine with a mouse / by John Burstein.
        p. cm. — (Math monsters)
      Summary: The four monsters are introduced to computers by Big Bill, who brings them
a package and instructions for hooking up and using what is inside.
      ISBN 0-8368-3817-3 (lib. bdg.)
      ISBN 0-8368-3832-7 (softcover)
      1. Computers—Juvenile literature. 2. Electronic data processing—Juvenile literature.
[1. Computers.] I. Title.
QA76.23.B87   2003
004—dc21
                                             2003045044

This edition first published in 2004 by
Weekly Reader® Early Learning Library
330 West Olive Street, Suite 100
Milwaukee, WI 53212 USA

Text and artwork copyright © 2004 by Slim Goodbody Corp. (www.slimgoodbody.com).
This edition copyright © 2004 by Weekly Reader® Early Learning Library.

Original Math Monsters™ animation: Destiny Images
Art direction, cover design, and page layout: Tammy Gruenewald
Editor: JoAnn Early Macken

Printed in the United States of America

1 2 3 4 5 6 7 8 9 07 06 05 04 03

You can enrich children's mathematical experiences by working with
them as they tackle the Corner Questions in this book. Create
a special notebook for recording their mathematical ideas.

Computers and Math
Electronic tools such as calculators and computers
are essential tools for teaching, learning,
and doing mathematics.

Meet the Math Monsters™

ADDISON

Addison thinks
math is fun.
"I solve problems
one by one."

Mina flies
from here to there.
"I look for answers
everywhere."

MINA

MULTIPLEX

Multiplex
sure loves to laugh.
"Both my heads
have fun with math."

Split is friendly
as can be.
"If you need help,
then count on me."

SPLIT

We're glad you want to take a look
at the story in our book.

We know that as you read, you'll see
just how helpful math can be.

Let's get started. Jump right in!
Turn the page, and let's begin!

One day, Big Bill came to the Math Monsters' castle.
He sang,
"I have a gift, here inside,
inside this box so big and wide.
It is a gift for everyone.
This gift will be a lot of fun."

"Wow!" said the monsters.
"Thank you. What is it?"
  "Try to guess," said Big Bill.
"Have fun!"
  Big Bill went back to his store.

Did you ever get a gift in a box and try to guess what it was before you opened it?

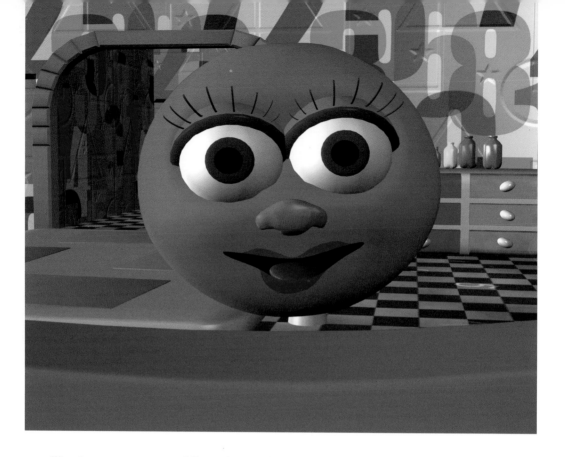

"Is it a new toy?" asked Split.

"Is it a big box of candy?" asked Multiplex.

"Let's bring it inside," said Addison.

Multiplex picked up the box.
"It is very heavy," he said.

What do you think could be in the box?

7

The monsters opened the box. They put the gift on the table.

"It is a new computer!" said Addison.

"How does it work?" asked Multiplex.

"Let's look in the box. Maybe there is something inside that can help us," said Mina.

What do you think the monsters will find in the box to help them?

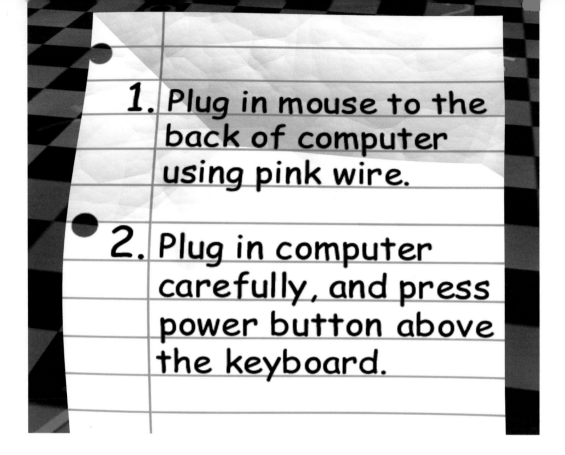

1. Plug in mouse to the back of computer using pink wire.

2. Plug in computer carefully, and press power button above the keyboard.

Inside the box, the monsters found a note.

"This note tells us what to do," said Split.

"First it says to plug in the mouse."

"Mouse?" asked Multiplex. "Is there a mouse in the computer? I will get some cheese to feed it."

Do you think that a computer mouse eats cheese?

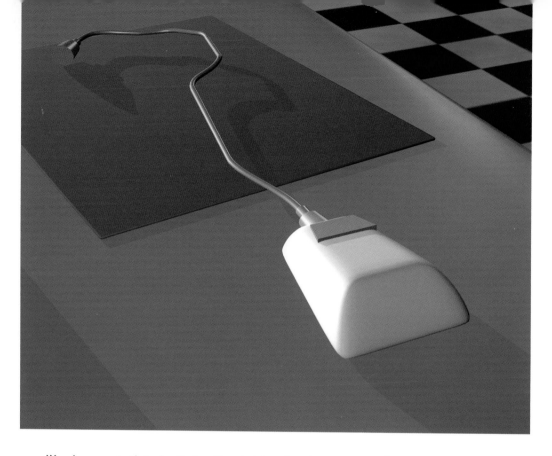

"I do not think it is that kind of mouse," said Split.

"I think it is this small white part," said Mina.

"It looks like a mouse with a long tail."

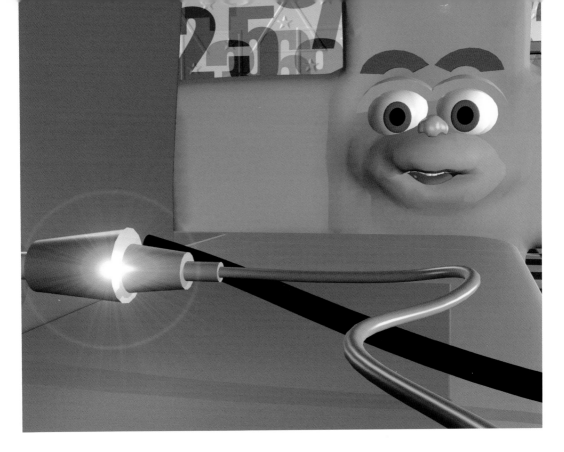

The monsters plugged the mouse into the computer.

"Now what?" asked Addison.

What do you think the monsters will do next?

"Now we need to plug in the computer," said Split. "We need to be very careful."

After they were done, Mina asked, "What is next?"

"The note says to press the power button on the keyboard," said Split.

"Keyboard?" asked Multiplex.
"I have keys to my truck, but I do
not see any keys on this computer."

*Do you know
what kind of keys
Split means?*

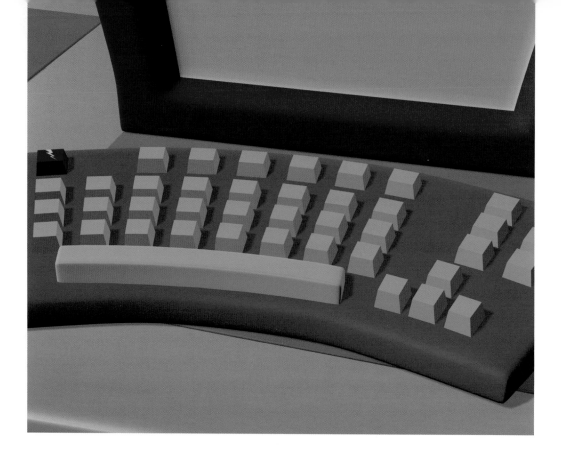

"This is the keyboard," said Addison. "These buttons are called keys."

"Where is the one that turns the computer on?" asked Mina.

"I think it is the red one," said Multiplex.

Multiplex pushed the red key.
The computer came on. The
monsters saw a picture of Big Bill
on the screen.

"This is the same as TV," said Mina.

How do you think a TV and a computer are alike? How are they different?

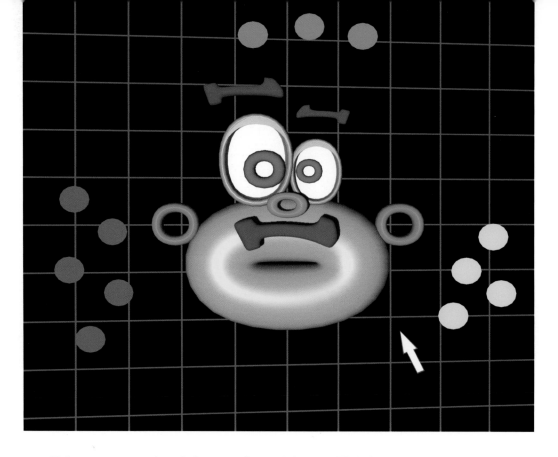

"You are right, Mina. It is like a TV, but you can do much more with a computer," said Big Bill.

"What can we do?" asked Split.

"How do we do it?" asked Addison.

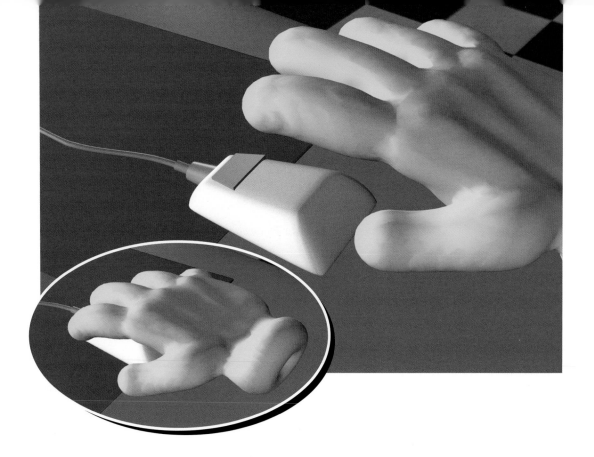

"First you must learn how to move the mouse and click the button," said Big Bill.

He showed them how.

"Now you can play games to help you learn," said Big Bill.

Have you ever played learning games on a computer? What kind?

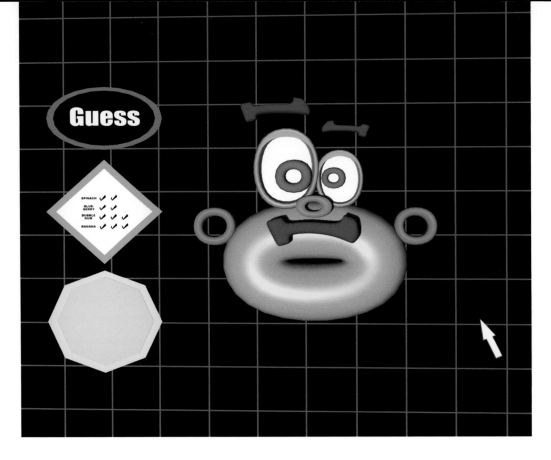

The monsters played lots of games. Some games helped them learn shapes. Some games helped them learn numbers. Some games were just for fun.

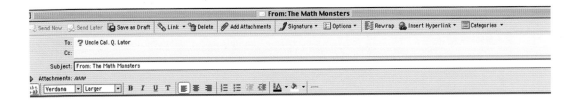

Send Now   Send Later   Save as Draft   Link ▾   Delete   Add Attachments   Signature ▾   Options ▾   Rewrap   Insert Hyperlink ▾   Categories ▾

To: ? Uncle Cal. Q. Lator
Cc:

Subject: From: The Math Monsters

Attachments: *none*

Verdana ▾ Larger ▾ **B** *I* U T ☰ ☰ ☰ ☷ ☷ ☷ ☷ A ▾ ▾

Dear Uncle Cal,

This is our first e-mail. Big Bill gave us a new computer and we are learning to use it.

How are you?

Love, Addison, Mina, Multiplex and Split

"You can also use the computer to send e-mail," said Big Bill.

"What is e-mail?" asked Mina.

"E-mail is mail that you send by computer," said Big Bill.

He showed them how to send a message.

Who would you send an e-mail to? What would you say?

21

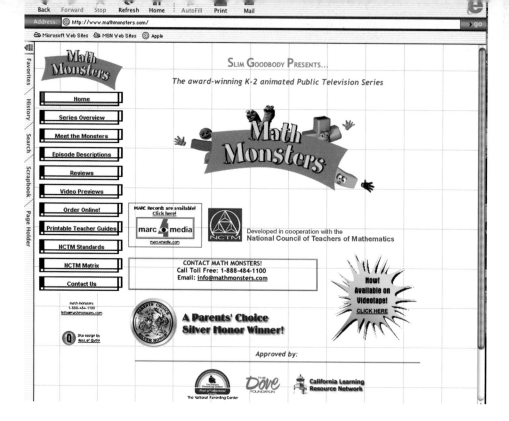

"You can use the computer to go on the Internet," said Big Bill. "You can find lots of things there."

"Can we learn about space?" asked Mina.

"Can we learn how bubble gum is made?" asked Multiplex.

"Sure," said Big Bill. "I will show you how to find what you want. It is called surfing the web."

Later, the monsters went outside. Their dog
Basehound took his turn. He played games.
He surfed the Internet. He sent an e-mail
to his sister Zip. It said,

    "A computer is such fun to use.
    It is a bow-wow tool
    for playing games
    and learning things
    and doing work for school."

*Would you
like to use a
computer? What
would you do?*

ACTIVITIES

Page 5 Talk with children about the clues they use when trying make an educated guess about what's inside a box. For example, they should take into account the size, shape, and weight.

Page 7 Help children use the clue that the box is heavy to guess what is inside. Talk about labels and how they provide information.

Page 9 Find directions that explain how to play a board game or assemble a toy. Talk about why these are helpful. Predict what might happen if there were no directions.

Pages 11, 13, 15, 17, 19 Even though children may be comfortable using a computer, they often don't know what the different parts do. Using a computer at home, at school, or at the library, lead children through the same steps the monsters take. Name and identify the hardware and important keys for operation. Practice using the mouse to manipulate objects on the screen.

Page 21 Help children send an e-mail to a friend or relative. Start with the name and e-mail address. Then write the message and send it.

Page 23 This is a great opportunity to explore the Internet in a supervised and instructional manner. Let children select a topic of interest. Support them as they conduct an Internet search on the topic. Collect and share addresses for favorite Internet sites. Have fun as you explore the uses of a computer.